Prospero's Bowl

Ken Head

Oversteps Books

First published in 2013 by

Oversteps Books Ltd
6 Halwell House
South Pool
Nr Kingsbridge
Devon
TQ7 2RX
UK

www.overstepsbooks.com

ISBN 978-1-906856-41-0

Printed in Great Britain by imprint digital, Devon

for Peggy, Kate & Charlie Newcombe,
finally together in the story

Acknowledgements:

Thanks are due to the editors of the following print and online magazines in which a number of the poems in this collection have appeared, though sometimes in slightly different versions:

Beat The Dust; Birds On The Line; Carillon; The Dawntreader; Envoi; 4th Dimension; The Indite Circle; Ink, Sweat & Tears; Inky Needles; The Journal; ken*again; Moodswing; Morning Star; Non-Euclidean Café; Obsessed With Pipework; The Ouroboros Review; Poems In The Waiting Room (New Zealand); The Poetry Kit (Caught In The Net); Poetry Monthly; Poetry SuperHighway; Purple Patch; The Ranfurly Review; Reach Poetry; Sarasvati; The Shine Journal; Snakeskin; Static Movement; Urban District Writer; The War Poetry Website.

Sus won the 2011 Cinnamon Press Micro-fiction Competition.
Hard Look, Safe As Houses and *Iron In The Soul* were included in Finding The Heart, a chapbook commended and placed 7th in the 2011 Indigo Dreams Press Winter Competition.
Walls Have Ears At Prinsengracht 263 was selected for Static Movement's 2010 anthology.

Contents

Passing Through 1
Inside The Frame 2
By Haweswater 3
Along Ashwell Road 4
Something To Measure Against 5
Misericordia 6
He Remembers Pluscarden 7
Stepping Off 8
Iron In The Soul 10
Canal: 2011 16
Prospero's Bowl 17
First Teacher 18
Sus 20
Seeing & Believing 21
Staying Power 22
1: Speaking Silence 22
2: Shadow Play 23
3: Chinese Whispers 24
4: Hell Money 25
5: Madam Chan 26
6: Off Limits 27
7: The Price Of Rice 28
8: On A Shoestring 29
9: Writing On The Wall 30
10: Buying Dragonware 31
A Slap In The Face 32
Hard Look 33
Upmarket Comes Expensive 34
Permanent Ways 35
In Our Garden Of Earthly Delights 36
from Bedrock 37
Compliance 38
Safe As Houses 39
Walls Have Ears At Prinsengracht 263 40
On The Road From Nam Dinh 41
Lady Of The Sorrows 42
Deep Focus 43
Prince Of Serendip 44

Comfortless: A Triptych 45
Taking A View 48
G-Cramps 49
Vegetable Knife 50
In Silence 51

Passing Through

In the morning early he walked down
the mountainside from the old village.
The narrow donkey track, winding serpentine
and stony across the slope of the land,
kept the glitter of the sea below dark cliffs
always in his eyes. He breathed in thyme
and the scent of fresh-cut grass where men
with scythes, who nodded quiet greetings
as he passed, had cleared the path while
he was still asleep and were resting then
in the dusty shade of ancient olive trees.
The spirit of the place hung in the air
like bee-filled midday heat and welcomed him,
a visiting stranger from another world.

Inside The Frame

In the museum, a woman is studying Studio Interior,
a painting by Benito Barrueta
She has been gazing into it for a long time.

It has the feel of a room that isn't used,
a space given over to dusty sunlight,
the dried-out husks of summer insects
along the window sill. Nothing challenges
the shadow-lines of easel, desk and chair
across the floor. A door left open
to let in laughter, movement, household
noise, a naked model, would be out of place.
The room's pristine, a humble harmony
of neat and unpretentious details.
There are no glasses, bottles, overflowing
ashtrays or plates of uneaten food,
no rumpled bed, no painter's technicolour
mess of dripping, squeezed-out tubes.

The life lived here is sober, still, meticulous
and hidden. Even the mirror's blank.
So, in the end, you work with what you have,
short brush-strokes that reference objects,
a rocking-chair, a footstool, paintings
in ornate, gilded frames around the walls,
a palette of finely graduated ochres,
greys with undertones of light that filter
through the window and negotiate the floor,
the ceiling, the air itself, thickening
shadows here, sharpening brightness there,
until, at last, the image settles,
becomes all at once clear and present
in a moment that feels suspended out of time.

By Haweswater

That there's no voice, not even birdsong, is what he notices,
that the silence remains untouched by any of the noise
he carries with him. Between the crunch of his boot soles
over stony ground and the pattern of his breathing,
he listens for it as he would the sound of waves along a beach
or wind through trees. Out of habit, he imagines the hubbub
he comes from, the journey he's made, the roaring torrent
of the motorways he's driven on, all there beyond the skyline.

The track he chooses cuts across the slope as if it knows the way.
Here and there, it forks, down to the lake, as cold and still
as a slab of polished jet, on past blocks of fenced-off conifers
where only shadows move behind the wire, uphill to the snow.
By a rock as big as a house he pauses, takes a break.
Years ago, he wouldn't have, but time's more powerful now
and landscapes like this, so filled with emptiness,
as mysterious as death. *No compromise*, they say, *keep moving*.

Along Ashwell Road

Rough and ready, canvas, branches,
makeshift bender.

In those days, it was a stretch of wild wood
way beyond the village. Left to badgers
mostly, overgrown, forgotten, a remnant
of neglected trees and deep, dark undergrowth
no one bothered with, it shawled itself
in separation like a gypsy woman
smoking her cheroot on the vardo steps
who doesn't enjoy being stared at.

He feeds the campfire,
wet wood, smoky,
she feeds the baby.

Travelling to work on a sunny morning,
it could seem a place to slip away to,
somewhere there might still be a secret door.
But in winter, frozen solid, snow-bound
and bleak as buggery on windy nights,
driving home with the heater going
full blast put romance back in perspective:
you wouldn't wish such misery on a dog.

On their uppers,
no one sees them, gone tomorrow.

Something To Measure Against

He follows in single file behind the village elders,
step by step up the rocky track, their sticks
tapping the way between banks of dusty bushes,
to the plateau at the top of the mountain
where the cistern is that gives water to homes
on his side of the island. Still early summer,
but already forty-plus before noon
and water's being rationed. Standing with them
as they unlock the observation manhole
and stare down into the dark to check the level,
their old men's leathery faces give nothing away,
except to show they understand how serious this is.

So why in God's name choose to live in a place
where the sun burns everything to dust and the fields
are full of stones? Even goats don't thrive here!
He already has his answers to these questions,
but stayed up all night watching shooting stars,
seeing how much whiter his house walls are
by moonlight than in the glare of the sun
and trying to explain them to himself again.
He remembers a story he must've read
somewhere about a child so impatient to know
if the seedlings he's planted are growing
that each day he pulls them up by the roots to check.

In his garden, too parched to enjoy before sunset,
which is when he'll eat, with mosquito coils
burning under the table, fruit fallen from trees
so blackened they might've been scorched by fire
lies drenched in its own sweet juices, rotting
slowly, a sticky feast that stains the ground
with landscapes only ants know how to travel.
Wasps festoon the air, sunlight's so fierce it scalds,
the cicadas' midday shrieking sounds demented,
like the rage of ghosts from home. No water now
until late afternoon and nothing to be done
but study patience. Nothing. A harder paradise.

Misericordia

We weren't supposed to walk the penitential way
to the shrine at the top of the mountain.
There were gigs and surreys with bright-painted wheels
waiting for us along the dock as we left the ferry.
The drivers smiled, gestured, called out best prices,
we could see the desperation in their faces.
But the horses were half-starved, callused, ribby,
their eyes and the sores on their legs both black with flies.
So tired to death they looked, we couldn't do it.

The priest-in-charge, a cheerful, suntanned man,
made no bones about it, he loved this tiny
church above the sea, his simple house knee-deep
in wild flowers, the view of paradise he shared
with God and the birds. *In this country,* he told us,
we have everything we need, except what we lack.

He Remembers Pluscarden

I came as a guest, and you received Me.
OSB. Rule of Benedict, Ch 53: On the Reception of Guests.

He stands among rows of wooden grave markers,
each with a brother's name, his date of birth
and death, nothing more, on a fine September afternoon.
Looking through trees along the valley, the abbey
is monks barrowing compost in a vegetable garden,
orchards of plum and apple trees laden with fruit,
unused beehives stacked against a wall and the sound
of one bell chiming. He feels time falling away.
At his back, no taller than a man, an effigy of pain
in chiselled oak tilts sideways in dry earth, a Calvary:
Christ crucified overseeing death's quiet corner.

They overwhelm him, these places of the soul,
make him feel, although he knows he must be wrong,
like grass that withers in the presence of a god.

Stepping Off

Dunster Woods on an afternoon in April.
Fog thick as woodsmoke from a damp bonfire,
clinging, silent, autumnal, the valleys
chock-full, no chance of the sun burning through.
Early on, a chilly white-out, ghostly ponies
standing sentinel in the mist, straggles
of blurry sheep tempting fate across the road.
Now, the scrunch of our boots over pine cones
and tree litter the only sound, we follow
our noses past well-intentioned finger-posts
through acres of regimented conifers
too lifeless to call woodland and too thick
with shadow to feel comfortable among:
the easy hikers' track to Bats Castle,
waiting for us up there inside the gloom.

It's a greenwood trail suffering ugly times,
muddy, puddled, tractor-rutted,
the only oak trees still putting up a fight
no more than parodies of themselves.
We keep an eye out for whatever might
be moving, pigeons, squirrels, a wide-winged
owl flapping tetchily out of our way,
a family of dark-brindled deer
stepping light as legend across the path.
There's nothing, though, even when we reach the moor,
that wilderness of yellow-flowering gorse
and heather snared in mist, where earthed-up
remnants of wall and the song of absence
in the air tell us people lived here once,
found their way in fog, like blind men, searching.

But to have begun here, pushing against life
and feeling it push back, struggling to work out
what's ahead, as a hunter does from tracks
in fresh snow, might not have seemed so hard
on sunny days, with skylarks, green valleys
and the ocean a morning's downhill walk

away through young forest. Making and mending,
hauling supplies, turning backbreaking
labour into food, must all have been grist
to the mill in the battle against failure
of belief, a deal with the gods that might make
the world more knowable, less pitilessly
harsh. Around the fire at night, hearts tuned
for signals from the dark, it's easy
to understand they'd put their faith in dreams.

Iron In The Soul

History could make a stone weep.

Marilynne Robinson: *Gilead*

1:

Walkers in Berghaus boots and North Face coats
come up here now, with their backpacks, thumb-sticks,
laminated O.S. maps and tourist notes.
At the top, they leave the litter from their picnics
and piles of dog crap inside plastic bags.

It's too easy a route when the weather's good,
a gentle couple of miles on signposted
Crown Estate tracks through what was an oak wood
once, though the survivors look exhausted
these days, arthritic, bony-fingered, skeletal.

The best time's when a real pea-souper sets in
and thousand-year-old spirits breathe down your neck.
That's when this ancient country comes alive again,
like a familiar you've been hoping might lift the sneck.

2:
Can't you just picture him testing the new grip
on his battle axe? A few flashy swings
to try the heft, relishing the limelight,
the wide-eyed girls going weak at the knees
in front of all that tattooed muscle,
a gaggle of snot-nosed, gawping lads,
watching him chop and slice through solid air,
asking themselves if he'll ever decide
they're men enough to start earning scars
like his, the savvy a warrior needs
to be a winner, instead of herding goats
all day and being frit to death at night
when they're left to guard the fires alone
with no mother moon to keep the dark at bay.

3:

It's thick, white fog they have in these parts, clings
like wet sheepskin. Not easy to defend against
when you can't see your nose in front of your face.

That's when raiders come, up through the forest,
taking their time over the climb, knowing
we're blind as bats until they're nearly on us.

Why they bother's the mystery, there's nothing
worth killing or dying for on this hilltop.
One or two pretty girls, maybe, but not much else.

You're surprised I'm here? It's a debt of honour.
These peasants found me badly wounded
and brought me back to life. I owe them everything,

although I still can't fathom why they fight so hard
to turn this stony patch of ground into a home.

4:

We were wanderers before we found this place,
homeless, friendless, always on the move,
living each day hand to mouth against the world.
Some of us died by the road and were left
not always buried. Others were born, but didn't
reach their naming. This was the way of it
and mustn't be forgotten. Today's a fine day,
though, even for an old woman with eyes so milky
she can't see across the valley. The sun's warm,
I can hear our bees getting busy on the gorse
and the sounds of laughter aren't a foolish dream.
There were times I wouldn't have believed
any place could be so kind, but this close
to being gone, I'm happy to know I was wrong.

5:

Felling clean timber. Hauling it in gangs.
Slave-labour all summer. Working like dogs
to get some kind of shelter up while we had
the weather. Wood-frames, straw-roofs,
nothing we thought would last, just digging in
for that winter. Enough to keep the wolf
from our doors. Somewhere to build a fire.

But defend ourselves against other people?
Why? We had no enemies, we were strangers
here. So we didn't start the wall till later,
after we'd learned the hard way that peace
of mind is harder to find than hens' teeth.
That wall surrounds the whole village now,
you can see, not that we ever let it hem us in.

6:

But for the wind-song through the gorse,
which tells no lies and offers up no secrets,
our place on these high hills is silenced now
as if it were a home bereft, left open
to the weather. What we sweated to make
of oak, with iron and stone to bind it fast
against the years, lasted not much longer
than a leaf will feed a moth. Strange to think
we're no more than travelling spirits
who won't again sleep anywhere on earth.
So many lives, so many deaths, all gone,
vanished into thin air. The lightest breeze
ruffling a child's hair, silvering a field
of grass, less than it takes to rattle a door.

Canal: 2011

There will be an after to be remembered ...
U. A. Fanthorpe: *Canal: 1977*

All morning, he's been discovering the towpath
between two waterways, the canal, silent
and still under tangled trees, keeping its story
to itself along with the silty ghosts
of the men who died digging it, and the river,
not much more than a trickle over stones
this time of year, its banks thick with nettles,
fireweed and the post-industrial wreckage
he's seen before in places no one uses
any more for sweating profit out of labour:
closed-down mills, tall-chimneyed factories,
an industrial waste disposal plant, tanks
overgrown with weeds, a row of cottages
too small to swing a cat, teetering dark
and narrow over the river, homes once,
but with roofs stripped now to make it hard
for squatters, and a nameless pub, *The Shannon*
& Chesapeake, maybe, *The Old Malt Shovel,*
The Jack House or *The Swan With Two Necks,*
finally up for sale. *No more local trade*
round here, you see. Physical graffiti
fenced off with razor wire and boarded up,
spelling out as clear as day what history means.

Prospero's Bowl

for Peter Hawthorn, woodcarver

... it was mine Art ... let thee out.
William Shakespeare: *The Tempest*, Act 1, Scene 2

Turned from a piece of venerable oak, it's a simple bowl,
a bare four inches wide, as cross-hatched,
grooved and whorled to give the grain its due
as leathery skin, but soft and warm as summer to the touch.

He offers it across his bench on an open palm as a piece
we might afford and silky with a final sheen
of oil, it sits there, rotund, unshowy,
glowing under the anglepoise like light before a storm.

In the lane, a tractor's grinding uphill towards the farm,
two collies bark from the bed of the cart
as it brushes a tangle of flowering elder overgrowing
the workshop window. *So what do we think?*

The bowl sits waiting. An acorn dropped a millenium ago
lies doggo, bides its time, finds room to breathe,
stays put during centuries of seasons while tides roll in
and history moves on. *Take me or leave me, I'm not in any hurry.*

First Teacher

Where shall we find the gateway to tomorrow?

What's hidden behind the crumbling, pock-marked wall, with its patches of stained cement, bare bricks and yards of cobwebbed cracks, is anybody's guess. It's much too tall to see above and doesn't offer clues. No doors, no sternly worded signs in different languages, no arrows pointing out the way to go. A neglected institution of the state? A hive of busy bureaucrats in suits, whose unseen labour oils the nation's wheels and keeps things running smooth as silk? An aristocratic palace left to rot or re-vamp by some real estate developer, some foreign billionaire or movie star who's into warehouses and lofts and just adores the chi-chi aphrodisiac of decaying splendour brought back to life by ultra-modern chic? Or who just gets off on *old*?

Half hidden by the shadows of the eaves, long rows of windows, recessed, barred and curtainless, suggest a prison or a nunnery with miles of worn magnolia paint, scrubbed floors that clack at regulated times and then stay dumb till someone walks on them again. Which is worse? Now there's a question. Not that the answer matters much to the gang of urchins on the derelict land nearby, who seem content to watch the cars pass, play their games, get on with life and leave things as they are. Except for one skinny, whey-faced girl with sagging socks, a grubby overcoat that doesn't fit and a snot-nosed boy in tow, who's probably her brother. From this distance, it's hard to be sure, but whatever she's doing, it's more serious than kicking a ball about or clambering over the carcasses of burned-out cars like a vandal claiming victory.

Absorbed, back turned to the world, using a lump of plaster as a stick of chalk, she's drawing a picture on the wall, writing words around it and saying them one by one, as if she needs to learn by heart something too important to forget. In spite of himself, the little boy's drawn in and starts to point, ask questions, look up at his sister's writing hand as if he thinks it's magic.

Which maybe it is. Eventually, as daylight wears thin and it starts to rain, the girl drops her makeshift chalk, brushes off her hands and steps back for a better view. Now the picture's done, it's clear she isn't bothered any more about forgetting and is ready to go home. But the boy reaches out towards it, says something, walks up to the wall and on tiptoe leans his ear against it as if he's listening for sounds. The girl laughs, skips away, calls out for him to come and makes to cross the road. After a puzzled second or two spent staring, he does as he's been told.

This is a house, this is a garden, these are the
fields where the children play.

Sus

Beyond the window
speed reduces landscape
to an afterthought.

Soldiers deployed beside the track, tanks slewed in an armoured chicane across a narrow road in the middle of nowhere. More than enough, you'd think, to warn us something wasn't right before our ***tgv*** throttled back to a resentful stop alongside a deserted forest halt too small to have a name. But nobody reacted until teams of men with scanners and laptops clambered aboard to check passports, slowly, carefully, giving out those small-hours, Cold War frontier vibes that make you wonder, if your memory stretches back that far, what it is they've already decided you've done.

Knowing the doors are locked doesn't help either, not if you're already as jumpy as he was, the man in the single window seat, travelling alone without much luggage. They barely glanced at his passport, dark green, elegant gold lettering on the cover, before they led him away, one of them carrying his bag and looking worried. There'd been no security check at Lausanne station, where we'd all got on, so nervous questions floated in the air.

After what seemed an age, they brought him back, watched as he struggled to stow his bag, then left him, humiliated, too shattered to face his own reflection in the window and as close as most men get to tears, to stew over whatever might've been said or done while they'd held him somewhere none of us could see.

For the rest of the journey, he seemed asleep, arms folded across his table, head down, barely moving until we arrived in Paris, where he disappeared, as we all did, quickly, onto the busy concourse. Looking for cover inside the crowd? Trying to blend in, as if he thought he must still be wanted for something?

In suspicious times
mistrust and fear
find everybody guilty

Seeing & Believing

There are fish in the water here, we say,
pointing down over the iron rail
and wondering whether it's sunlight
or nature's magic that colours them pale
gold beneath a net of seaweed so bright
and fine it has the look of filigree.
Like glittering torpedos, they move fast,
sensing our shadows and flitting away,
long, slim bodies more difficult to see
than half-remembered faces from our past.
Wind gently ruffles the silvered surface,
not much, but enough to confuse our eyes
and leave us staring at an empty space,
almost convinced that our senses tell lies.

Staying Power

... not time's blank spaces ...
Lee Tzu Pheng: *Re-semblances*

1: Speaking Silence

Like people, some stories last, others fade
too fast for comfort and these days,
done up to the nines the way it is, all sanitized
glitz and photo opportunities for tourists,
you might think Chinatown's a different place.

But you'd be wrong. Only fools and schemers
think the past is dead and theirs to bury.
Memories don't vanish like graffiti
under coats of paint, they bide their time,
like acorns, waiting centuries to grow, lying

quiet, knowing there's strength in readiness
and patience, the slow pulse of history
drowsing in dusty rooms, cooking mee siam
with egg and sambal for hungry families,
hearing the slap of mah-jong tiles at midnight.

2: Shadow Play

They're the air we breathe. We cut our teeth
on them, stories of opium fortunes
lost in fires, the gold, the gambling dens,
young girls shipped over in boatloads
to work the brothels, misers half-starved
in their own homes, surrounded by wealth
they daren't spend. My wife who died.
The blind hawker kids rob, market-traders
forever slaving to fill the rice bowl.
That's the kind of stuff people want to hear.

At funerals, we burn the universe, giant
Heaven and Earth joss sticks that last.
Stiltwalkers leap through fire, do acrobatics,
make sure our spirits live to tell their tales.

3: Chinese Whispers

Don't let all that tourist bullshit fool you,
there are still hungry ghosts in every house,
shadows waiting in forgotten rooms
for the chance to take up where they left off
or get out from under a lifetime's pain
when the gates between worlds are opened.
There's old Yeo, who hand-paints paper lanterns
delicate as flowers, that contractor
with crafty eyes who chews on the butt
of a soggy cheroot all day and pays
rock-bottom rates when times are hardest,
the bar-girls, nameless, with bone-white faces,
who chat together when they have the time
and their pimps, as ever was, at daggers drawn.

4: Hell Money

Cash to burn. Bundles of fake bank-notes
piled along rows of shelves at the back
of the shop. Billions in non-toxic,
inflation-proof, platinum-rated
underworld hush money, a joss-paper
king's ransom, payola to sweeten the gods.
Celestial kick-backs, rhinos, baksheesh
by the barrow-load, spondulicks, shekels,
smackers, tosheroons, a sou, a widow's mite,
the universal get-out-from-under
for the ghosts of the venerated dead,
down-payment on a pardon for their sins,
a bit of old-time magic to soothe their souls
and all of it food to feed a hungry fire.

5: Madam Chan

Peering out from behind the window-bars
of a dismal death-house down Sago Lane
where the dying sleep in their coffins
if they can afford one, besoming bad luck
off the five-foot way before the first customer
calls in for Gold Coin mooncakes or a chat,
selling Chinese pomeloes lorried down
from Ipoh, or glistening *ikan selar*
in aluminium bowls, she's a hard worker,
eats raw fish and chili with her porridge
at a place across the street from Hup Kiat's,
where they make the best *popiah* skins
in Chinatown and always says her prayers
at the altar of the God of Heaven.

6: Off Limits

We are as we are, they say, *and don't forget it,*
we're not about to explain ourselves to you.
These are people who live life unobserved
and separate. Even in broad daylight,
a walk among the ginnels, the unsigned
alleys that lead to decrepit godowns,
back-lane metal workshops and hawker stalls
you wouldn't risk, where men talk money
till the cows come home, will get you noticed.
What's a foreigner with a camera doing here?
You're in a private world of padlocks, bolts
and shutters, a clannish neighbourhood
where there are rules, where you'll feel the eyes,
the faces set and watchful, the sudden silence.

7: The Price Of Rice

You live here, yes, work for gov'ment, okay?
English, yes? You have big job, earn plenty?
No, no, is okay. Can, can, I un'stan'.
This good place so long you all time work har'.
I work ev' day, no take holiday, only
maybe New Year, go back home see fam'ly
few days. Have wife and childs so must go back
sometime. Take bus, take other bus. Ver' long.
I buy this taxi, but not mine yet, b'long
still finance company, so cannot use
for own. Have good friend who drive when I not
or sick sometimes. Is okay. He honest.
We help one 'nother all time. Must do, right?
Both us know how man' cents make one dollar.

8: On A Shoestring

Leaning over her barrow, she counts her takings,
all the money she has in the world, then casts
an experienced eye over the bananas
already spoiling in the heat, their skins
turning brown and soft. She'll never sell them.

She wills away the fear squeezing her chest,
checks the roll of notes again, wondering
if she'll be able to eat and pay her rent.
It's lucky she doesn't need much. A bed's
enough, somewhere to rest and remember.

If she dies tonight while the city's asleep
it'll be a blessing. She chuckles and spits.
The world's a stupid place, full of suffering
and pain. Better not to have been born at all.

9: Writing On The Wall

His stand-up desk and wobbly stool, the pens
and brushes, the bottles of ink are gone,
as he is, forever, but accept this,
acknowledge the iron-clad will of the world
and strips of rich-red paper may still hang
from wooden clothes-pegs on lengths of wire
across the wall outside the scribe's house
in Trengganu Street, their golden characters
for health and harmony, calligraphy
designed to bring prosperity and luck
a little closer, still glitter when they catch
the sun like flashbacks to a time *before*,
a life so far away and gone for good
it's more difficult to bring back every day.

10: Buying Dragonware

They bring it to the counter piece by piece
from wooden packing cases out the back,
each item swathed in newsprint and trailing
straw. There's reverence in the unwrapping,
the whisking away of dust, their careful
check for imperfections, plates and dishes
being held unhurried up to the light
and murmured over between themselves
just in case. This early, the street
is cool and quiet, we have the shophouse
to ourselves and it teaches us: the slow
back and forth shuffle of Ah Kow and his wife,
the abacus clicking, a fan whirring,
our sense of buying something that will last.

A Slap In The Face

Late one hot night, two cars, engines racing,
half-cut male voices shouting the odds:
young guns setting the world ablaze,
seven of them standing wide-legged, laughing,
enjoying a communal piss against our wall.

Next night, they're back under the street-lamp,
checking darkened doorways by the light
of mobile 'phones, flicking dog-ends into bins
to start a fire. It's after three before they go,
too late for a few hours sleep to be much help.

In daylight, one plastic wheelie-bin's a stump
of wax. There's ash on the bin-store floor
where they've tipped out piles of garbage
and made a bonfire. Blocks of flats like ours,
the police say, need to be made more secure.

Better prevention, fewer problems. It's our call.
Maintenance cleans up, replaces the bin,
the smell of disinfectant lingers. But that night
they come again, to the car-park this time.
Three cars damaged, one taken and driven away.

All summer this goes on and with it appears
something we haven't known before.
Where it's from and where it hides on the rare
quiet nights is like asking where bad smells
go when the window's open, where torchlight

disappears to at the end of the beam. No words
we're familiar with explain it. A way's been
found into our lives we've never thought to bar,
a forgotten door that lets in fear and rage,
marauding beasts, uncompromising, vengeful.

Hard Look

Past lines of cars and vans parked nose-to-tail
on both sides of the street, past newish blocks
of low-rise flats and maisonettes, balcony
railings post-box red, wires from *Sky* dishes
hanging loose down walls stained soapily
by bathroom overflows, the path divides:
left, to a take-away and the new mosque,
straight on to a fenced-in five-a-side pitch.

A man starting a kick-about with his son
is carefully pushing the ripped-up wings
and carcase of a pigeon out through a hole
in the wire with his foot. *Rats,* he explains
to the child, *It must've been killed by rats,
some time last night while you were fast asleep.*

Upmarket Comes Expensive

French-kissing over their cappuccinos
outside the corner café, two pierced,
tattooed and shaven-headed girls intent
on one another don't notice the dog
rub mangy flanks hard against a piss-stained,
concrete wall to ease the itch, then shake off
pain and trot across to sniff their boot soles
one by one from underneath the table.

Three floors above, labourers shovelling
broken brick and plaster into a long,
blue chute dangling like plastic intestine
down the front of a gutted tenement
stop to have a laugh, enjoy the show, spit
out the dirty taste of dust and decay.

My children were all born in this room,
there were no maternity hospitals
then, and it was here I nursed my husband
till he died. We laid him out on our bed
the best we could while the men went looking
for a doctor who'd come in the middle
of the night. I don't know what I'd have done
without such good neighbours. That's how it was
in those days, we stuck together because
we had to. It would be easier for me
now, though, to go into a home. No more
stairs to manage, no shopping to carry,
kinder to my legs. But I won't. A bit
more pain's not going to hurt at my age.

Permanent Ways

He doesn't appreciate seeing them close up,
migrant field-workers huddled
against the hedge, clothes stuck to them
in the rain, not while he's eating,
making the most of his free upgrade.

In the past, when he's made this trip,
he's always enjoyed the views
across fields that looked perfect,
groomed, the way farms do in stories.

But what sticks in his craw this time
isn't that, the driving rain, or even
the gangmaster's muddy Transit
bogged down at the edge of the field,

it's something else, something disturbing
that sets him wondering, the way a jolt
or high-speed lurch across a set of points
will do, what state the subgrade's in,
whether the ties and ballast might be shifting.

In Our Garden Of Earthly Delights

To think we buy gowns lined with ermine
For dolts that can't or won't determine
What's best to rid us of our vermin!

Robert Browning: *The Pied Piper Of Hamelin*

From the top of the hayloft ladder, a rat
the colour of rotting timber staring
down at him as he reaches for the next rung,
the concentrated, feral eyeballing,
fearless, hostile, ready for anything,
that more than sixty years ago made fear
cry out and his arms almost lose their grip
on all the time he's had to live since then.

There've been other encounters with rats:
a moiling mass of them scavenging
uncollected plastic garbage bags
outside a restaurant; a single file
of scrawny, soot-black individuals
slipping through a crack in the tunnel wall
of an Underground station like skulking,
low-life criminals on the run from justice.

Not that they have it easy. He's seen them
trapped and spitting in metal cages,
finished off by dogs, skewered with forks,
their leathery hides stuck to the road
like patches of infected skin, and once,
one Big Daddy of a buck rat still alive
and kicking between the jaws of a python.
Nature in the raw, blood-red in tooth and claw.

from **Bedrock**

From a safe distance, because our nervous
guide doesn't want to risk going closer,
we stare towards the beach through razor wire.

They use inner tubes or home-made oil-drum
rafts and this is where the current drives them.
If they're lucky and don't choose a moonless
night to cross, a patrol boat might find them
before the sharks. Some survive, but flotsam
and jetsam here are the stuff of nightmare.

Those who make it in one piece are sent back.
Amputees follow when they can travel.
Freedom gets more expensive every day.

Compliance

Your turn's coming, you can see it ahead,
at the other end of the line of cars
stalled by the barrier in driving rain
while troops in hooded capes the same drab green
as the bush slosh through potholes of rust-red
laterite run-off and point their guns
at the driver next in line for the slow
once-over, the cold-eyed document check.

Peering in through your rolled-down windows,
they silence the world with question marks:
will they let you go? Back-seat passengers
stay silent. You're waved towards barbed-wire
fencing, a red-and-white-checked metal gate,
heavy machine-guns mounted on tripods
under cover in the backs of jeeps.
A soldier ticks his clipboard, signals you

on, grins as you pull obediently
away and the gate drops back into place.
No one puts his foot down, you drive slowly,
line astern, like undertakers, mindful
of frailty and watchful of the road.
The saturated green landscape melts by
outside, leaves you hungry for tarmac,
white lines, the false security of road signs.

Safe As Houses

What we see has meaning
becomes memory
grows larger than life.

We were standing just across from them
outside Arrivals, the two of us,
like everybody else in the long queues
for buses to the airport car parks,
finding space for ourselves inside the crush,
watching our bags, noticing a chill
in the air again, cracking worn-out jokes
and sharing stories with total strangers
the way you do, but all the time thinking
of getting home, turning our door key
in a lock we knew would open. The one thing
nobody jokes about, because it matters.

They were wearing soot-black combat fatigues,
body armour, boots that gave them the look
of storm-troopers and they were armed:
hand-guns, batons, snub-nosed automatic
weapons with pistol grips, a long-barrelled
sniper rifle with telescopic sights,
the kind of mailed-fist warning you can't avoid
seeing on the streets of other countries,
places you wouldn't choose to call your own.
Invisible behind dark glasses, their eyes
gave us a once-over as they passed,
one muttered something, the others grinned.

Tar them all with the same brush
dead simple
wink when you call it freedom

Walls Have Ears At Prinsengracht 263

We have to whisper and tread lightly during
the day, otherwise the people in the warehouse
might hear us.

Anne Frank's diary: *July 11th, 1942.*

It's cold for the time of year, I know, but we like
to leave the warehouse doors open. After all,
we just grind and pack spices all day, we've nothing
to hide. Except maybe our curiosity. There's enough
bread delivered here most days, you know, to feed
a large family, even though the place is empty
once we clock off. It's odd, you've got to admit.
The cleaning woman's noticed, too. Thinks
there must be people hiding upstairs somewhere.
Says she's heard noises coming from behind
the cupboard by the storeroom. Coughs and whispers,
people walking about. Claims she heard a girl
laughing one morning just like young Miss Anne.
Mind you, she's a nasty piece of work that one,
if ever there was, always nosing around
where she didn't ought to. Anything she told me,
I'd take with a very large pinch of salt!
What was she doing up there in the first place,
I'd like to know. She'll make trouble
before she's much older, mark my words.
Drop us all in it, probably. Then what'll we do?
It's all right for her, but I've got kids to feed,
I need this job, so I wouldn't trust her, not as far
as I could spit against a gale! Safer to keep
your thoughts to yourself these days. I tell her so.
No knowing where you might end up if you don't.
My name? Now why would you want that?
I'm nobody, really. I just work here, that's all.
One of the hired hands, you might say.

On The Road From Nam Dinh

i.m. Robert Capa (1913 – 1954)

They're so alike in age they could be brothers,
but what draws me into the photograph
isn't only the body in the dirt
at the side of the track, a young man's,
half-naked, barefoot, arms tied out of sight
behind him, one side of his skull a mess
of pulp and blood, a battlefield execution
if there ever was one, or the soldier
wearing baggy fatigues and dark glasses,
pistol and grenades hung from his belt,
a sub-machine gun slung across his chest,
who's staring down at the corpse and seems
to be smiling, as if the danger's over
and he feels safe enough to drop his guard.

It's what's set to happen in the background,
beyond where the road's being swept
for mines and a platoon's wading thigh-deep
through an undulating sea of grass
as harmless as the day is long. The moment's
crystal clear: men walking and talking
together, side by side, weapons shouldered,
chinstraps loose, body language relaxed,
the grinding discipline of fear stood down.
Only the photographer's still hankering
after action, the one shot he hasn't taken yet.
He moves, a better angle, loads new film,
changes *f*/stop, shutter speed, checks the sun,
takes the step there are no words to describe.

A boot treads down soft earth
pressure plate
anti-personnel mine.

Lady Of The Sorrows

I looked over Jordan and what did I see...?
Wallis Willis: *Swing Low, Sweet Chariot*

Winter in the village. Devastation the backcloth.
Hunger gnawing even the dreams of the sick.
The man with the camera confronts ruin,
hunts down the killing image, keeps his focus,
shoots roll after roll of film while daylight lasts:
it's cold-eyed clarity that does the damage, nails
the crime, not sentiment. That much he knows.

When he finds her among the rubble of a house,
abandoned, dumbstruck, frozen into grief,
her face a wide-eyed, catatonic scream, she can't
take in a word he says, is with her children
and her husband, dead. She's incoherent, babbles,
tells him angels will come soon to take her home.
He photographs her, what else should he do?

Deep Focus

Keep a green bough in your heart ...

A shaven-headed boy carrying a basket over one arm
the way a woman does when she goes to market
walks barefoot along the railway track. It's spring,
a sunny April afternoon, no gunfire, no bombing.
Like the birds pecking for food in the dirt, he feels safe.

There's a shout, someone calling. The boy looks round,
then flinches away, a man standing on a bogie flat
is pointing a camera at him. He makes to run, doesn't
want his likeness stolen by a foreigner in uniform
now the war's as good as over, but changes his mind.

The man looks harmless, after all, and he'll have cash
in his wallet, they always do, so maybe he'll want
a memento to take home. Metal belt buckles, badges
and buttons he's cut off the kit of dead soldiers,
a cigarette case or a lighter. He has plenty of stuff,

good souvenirs. Still taking pictures, the man moves
across the goods yard towards him. He imagines
smiling, gets ready to hold out his basket. With luck,
there'll be food tonight. He waits and watches,
tries to stay calm. One step at a time's good walking.

... and the singing bird will come. *

* Chinese proverb

Prince Of Serendip

His face in shadow, his back to a pillar, the child
sits cross-legged on the tiled floor,
a sheet of plastic between his body and the cold.
Around him, there's debris, less than you'd expect
in a building, in this case a mental hospital,
that's been shelled for five days, but enough.
There seems to be nobody else around, no staff,
no patients, but absorbed in what he's doing,
the puzzle he's trying to resolve,
that sense of stricken abandonment
observers like us might be sure he's feeling
doesn't show itself. If anything, he seems lost
to whatever else may be going on,
as perhaps only children are wise enough to be.
Laid out neatly in front of him, as precisely
as they might be in a museum or a science lab,
are ten jagged-edged fragments, shards of pottery,
splinters from the casing of an exploded round,
in the gloom what we're seeing isn't easy to fathom,
so to be certain, we have to do the impossible,
sit down beside him and wait for it all to make sense.

Comfortless: A Triptych

1:
What should he tell them? That their utopia
had been his once? That like some poet
hiding from reality, he'd shared their vision
of a peaceful country not beset by violence?

He hides his nervousness. The fierce young men
around him on the grass, two dozen or so
of them, will be expecting something special
from him in the way of leadership and wisdom,

as do the watchful party minders at the back
who'll report him if he doesn't toe the line,
or shoot him. That's why they've sent him here,
forgetting he's just a worn-out academic

from a university closed down for subversive
teaching, not some kind of visionary thinker
or prophet whose words will help the struggle,
jump-start trouble, spark off the revolution.

In his mind, he runs through what he'll say
and how he'll say it. Worn-out ideology,
political claptrap. Don't they understand?
People want iPhones, credit cards and comfort.

2:

There he is, there, right in front of the house,
her last son, still a child, lying dead
between the bodies of a piglet and a chicken,
pets he ran to rescue from the bullets.

She can still hear the soldiers yelling at him
in the seconds before they opened fire
and cursing her a few minutes later,
when they moved on, for being so stupid.

For being a bad mother. Her worst nightmare.
As if the cholera women fear even more
than the evil eye and pray to the gods
to keep their children safe from isn't enough.

An old woman she doesn't know hurries by
clutching a wooden box to her chest.
More of her neighbours will straggle back soon
from the foxholes they've dug in the fields.

She should've done the same, although now
she's alone, with nobody to help bury her boy,
how she'll survive, what becomes of her,
hardly seems worth troubling herself about.

3:
The leader and his wife are immaculate,
as confident of their cutting edge
as burnished steel blades. They're unique
even now, in their moment of defeat.

From behind a barricade of microphones,
they smile and glitter for the press,
she in her trademark designer suit and he,
the generalissimo, in a uniform bedecked

with braid and unearned battle honours.
He speaks. 'What's to become of us?
A difficult question. There will, of course,
be many changes, a period of transition.

It will be a testing time, a time of sacrifice.
This is why my wife and I are leaving
today for Washington, London and Paris.
Peace with honour is our goal, but the talks

may be protracted.' Outside, the rotors
of the presidential helicopter sound
impatient. The entourage begins to shuffle
off, to a wealthy life in exile, unforgiven.

Taking A View

About pain, the black-shawled women know enough
to last a lifetime: that anything may happen
at any moment, that good men not home by nightfall
may never be seen again, that a child's cry,
a screech of brakes, may bring the curtain down
forever. The fingers telling beads are wise with hurt.

They sit together in a corner of the square and watch
as lines of men take on, barehanded, the task
of shifting tons of stone and rubble. Even the worst
that can be thought must somehow be got through.
A three-legged dog barks crazily at pigeons
it can't chase, bar girls not dressed for rescue work

look the other way, children, who know the words
to all their songs, are playing skipping games
across the street and someone nearby is barbecueing
meat. Mouths water. Garlic, hot charcoal. Guilt.
The women understand the pattern these things make,
they expect no sudden miracle. They are old, not fools.

G-Cramps

In size order, a whole set. The biggest,
cast iron, four or five foot long,
like wide-jawed, monopod monsters
waiting to be fed, stood propped
against the workshop wall. The rest,
right down to the smallest, a bare
six inches, hooked underneath a shelf.

There were no Allen keys, only throat-catching,
home-made glues brewed patiently
over slow burners for days, to hold together
mortise and tenon joints cut perfectly
(because nearly was never good enough)
by hand. Then, finally, the G-cramps,
gripping the finished piece from all angles

while the glue set, jaws kept away from sleek
sapele, white oak or beech by small, flat
off-cuts saved for the purpose. Too much
tension twisted the joints, too little left them
loose. Only my father's craftsman's eye
and hand on cold, indifferent metal
understood the measure of the difference.

Vegetable Knife

Its wooden handle's worn, stained dark with use,
the stubby blade re-sharpened year on year,
yet when I find it, forgotten in the kitchen drawer
along with spoons, tea-strainer, all those odds
and ends left useless now, I have to touch it,
feel against my hand, as weighty as a life,
the heavy presence of the past, see the grain
run true round metal rivets and, along the blade,
still visible, just about, *Firth Stainless,*
The Stainless Cutlery Company, Sheffield,
and there's my no-nonsense mother, aproned
at the kitchen sink, peeling vegetables
for her family's Sunday lunch, a band-aid
round her finger where this knife had slipped and cut.

In Silence

After Utagawa Hiroshige: *A man crossing a bridge in a snowy landscape.*

An old monk, head down, shoulders hunched against thick, wet
snow, hobbles across a rickety wooden bridge.

Chilled to the bone, bad leg giving him gyp,
nose running like a tap, he hasn't spared a thought
for his Buddha nature since the cold shivered
him awake in the small hours.

For the umpteenth time, he sniffs, curses
his luck, wonders what he did years ago to have
ended up where he is now, then tells himself
to forget about it till he's home.

Life's easier to fathom, he's decided, after a hot meal
by a good fire than when you're struggling with it in the cold.

Oversteps Books Ltd

The Oversteps list includes books by the following poets:

David Grubb, Giles Goodland, Alex Smith, Will Daunt, Patricia Bishop, Christopher Cook, Jan Farquarson, Charles Hadfield, Mandy Pannett, Doris Hulme, James Cole, Helen Kitson, Bill Headdon, Avril Bruton, Marianne Larsen, Anne Lewis-Smith, Mary Maher, Genista Lewes, Miriam Darlington, Anne Born, Glen Phillips, Rebecca Gethin, W H Petty, Melanie Penycate, Andrew Nightingale, Caroline Carver, John Stuart, Ann Segrave, Rose Cook, Jenny Hope, Christopher North, Hilary Elfick, Jennie Osborne, Anne Stewart, Oz Hardwick, Angela Stoner, Terry Gifford, Michael Swan, Denise Bennett, Maggie Butt, Anthony Watts, Joan McGavin, Robert Stein, Graham High, Ross Cogan, Ann Kelley, A C Clarke, Diane Tang, Susan Taylor, R V Bailey, Alwyn Marriage, John Daniel, Simon Williams, Kathleen Kummer, Jean Atkin, Charles Bennett, Elisabeth Rowe and Marie Marshall.

For details of all these books, information about Oversteps and up-to-date news, please look at our website:

www.overstepsbooks.com